What?

Baptists, Fun~~~~~~~~~~~~~~ Orthodox Jewish believers are right: The Bible may be seen as Literal Truth. The World could have been created, fossils and all, in 7 days.

How?

He may have programmed it out of Fractals. 3-D Fractals. In the beginning was the Word. What we see are the echoes. Fractals, building blocks of building blocks.

Why?

Traditional Roman Catholics are right: We have Free Will. So, Creation had to be made in such a way that we could never prove or disprove that He made it. How else could we have Free Will?

When?

For all we know, 5,000 or 10,000 years ago. Things like fossils, Carbon 14 and sedimentary rocks may have been programmed in place with 3D Fractal shapes.

"Bill Adams' theory of Multi-Dimensional Fractals can help to bridge the gap between Science and the Bible's account of Creation."

Kenneth Fisher, Chairman
Concerned American Roman Catholics

"The more original a discovery, the more obvious it seems afterwards."

Arthur Koestler
On Ideas

WARNING – DISCLAIMER:

Throughout the long succession of miracles that make up the Jewish and Christian Faiths of our Fathers, professionals have been provided to give guidance.

Salvation is not a do-it-yourself project. Simply reading this, or any book, is no guarantee. Professional help from ordained, traditional clergy can be a great help.

Seek no guidance from anyone who does not believe that God is capable of miracles. If, at Judgment, we are denied admittance to Heaven, it will be, to some degree, because we did not bother to select a good Guide.

Old Drum Publishing
Box 401
Portersville, PA 16051

Order forms and Reader's Comments in back of book.

First printing March 1997
9 8 7 6 5 4 3 2

Library of Congress Catalog Card #: 97-091645

ISBN 0-9639623-1-0

100% USA

Beginning a new philosophy is simple: just come up with a view of the world, the details of which hang together and can't be contradicted.

If, after reading *My Yoke is Easy, and My Burden is Light. . .*
A Current Technology Translation of the Bible, you wish to send a
Reader's Comment for possible inclusion in the next edition, please
use Reader's Comment Blanks behind order forms in back of book.

Order information is in back of book.
Old Drum Publishing, Box 401,
Portersville PA 16051
Or call 1-800-OLD DRUM (653-3786)

My Yoke is Easy, and My Burden is Light . . .

(A Current Technology Translation of the Bible)

William E. Adams

Old Drum Publishing
Portersville, PA

It's all come together,
and it all makes sense.

　　My Yoke is Easy, and My Burden is Light...

My Yoke is Easy
and My Burden (is) Light

Matthew 11:30 is one of the most fascinating passages in the Bible. An obvious meaning is: "The task I have for you fits your abilities. The burden I give you is easily carried."

Reading the passage in light of a Current Technology Translation shows a tiny bit of how much more there is to it. Most of us don't know much about Iron Age technology, so we don't fully understand Scriptural passages that relate to things like yokes. Today, Bible translations are all linguistic or political in origin, rather than technical.

Bible translators churn out translation after translation. The more linguistically correct a new Bible is, the more out-of-touch it is with under-educated moderns than the one before. Few people today know in detail what a "yoke" is, let alone what an amazing revolution it caused.

People can't believe Scripture if they don't relate to it. As the Information Age progresses, fewer people can relate to a Bible that's linguistically perfect but technologically out of date. Today, who knows a shepherd? Who has sheared a sheep?

Only a few thousand non-Amish Americans know how to yoke a team, connect it to a wagon, mill, pump, or plow, and do useful work with it. To get the real meaning of the passage, we can either describe more accurately what a yoke is, or we can use new terminology that may give fuller meaning to the passage.

If moderns are to believe, the Bible must be translated in a way that relates to current technology, as well as be faithful to the meaning of the Author.

Sometimes, Try Taking it Literally.

When we want to see what a Bible Passage means, we should try taking the words literally, no matter how ridiculous that may seem. Give the Author credit for being smart enough to choose words that would fit all times. It's often helpful to assume initially that His words are literally true. When you read "My yoke is easy, my burden light.", consider that one obvious meaning of those words for today is: "I have a perfectly fitting yoke that helps me carry light."

My Yoke is Easy . . .

"It better be!" would be a response from people who knew how heavy and uncomfortable a yoke could be. Every single Iron Age person knew that a yoke was a wooden harness put on an animal or slave to increase output. They knew how bizarre it would be for people who weren't forced to wear a yoke to even think about putting one on. A Current Technology Translation lets us see that "Who does this Jesus think He is, expecting us to be yoked!" would be the usual response.

From before the Year One, our ancestors were mostly animal-powered Iron-Agers. The very newest Bible translations have more meaning to them than to moderns. Where there is familiarity with the things in the Bible, there is more belief in it because its relevance is more obvious. That's why the most faithful communities are in rural areas. Within living memory, farmers still worked with animal-powered equipment.

Power Transfer Devices

Since few moderns are aware of the importance of a yoke, they don't see many of the meanings in a Scripture passage based on allusions to such a device. Today, a person powered by nuclear and/or fossil fuels would see a yoke, if he knew what one was, as just another power-transfer device.

"My yoke is easy" could be better understood by a Mechanized Modern if it said: "My infinitely variable transmission is made of ultra-light aircraft aluminum. Each of its parts are always perfectly and automatically meshed to match the speed, tire size, load variations, road changes, power variations, and vehicle weight to provide maximum output." In other words, The Modern would understand that something truly miraculous was being discussed.

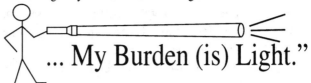

... My Burden (is) Light."

When the Bible was written, light as applied to burden referred to reduced weight. Today, Moderns can see a different meaning. Today, we apply light to energy. A laser-using engraver moves rays of nearly pure light around every single day. Such a person could reasonably say, "My burden is light." From neon sign makers to light bulb designers to power plant workers to laser surgeons, lots of people carry a burden that is literally light.

Jesus can be imagined shrugging nonchalantly while saying: "The fisherman pulls in his net. The policeman carries his gun. The mason moves his bricks. The porter carts his luggage. As for me, my burden is light. I can use what I carry to move everything from mountains to sub-molecular particles in the minds of men."

Things Seen and Unseen

A Current Technology Translation gives us a glimpse of His power that we can understand. Today, we know better than ever that light is a refined thing of great power, and that it is only a tiny part of the entire Energy Spectrum. A

Current Technology Translation implies that He carries the entire Energy Spectrum, not just the visible part.

He could carry both light and the formula for making light. We can only crudely imitate His light when our most advanced technicians cut unwanted cells away with surgical lasers or build up sub-molecular structures with nano-meter wavelength lasers that deposit atoms.

When He says "My burden is light.", today we get a better idea of His awesome power than ever before, an idea that must be further explored.

Looking At Light

Current Technology Translation shows us that the burden can be light, itself, as from the sun or a laser. We also see a tiny example of God's foresight/power because both meanings of the word He chose have meaning, though completely different, to people living thousands of years and miles apart.

Light also means "not dark". Souls that are stained and spotted with sin are darkened. When He says "My burden is not dark", He is also referring to his own burden. He is telling us very emphatically that He is not carrying any sin of His own along with Him. If we want to excuse any sort of sin, we cannot find even the slightest excuse to do so in His teaching.

Light also means "clear", as in: "It is clear, there is no

confusion." In His teachings, it is clear that there is not the slightest shadow of doubt.

Light as Economic Efficiency

In all generations, light as applied to load also means "economic efficiency". An ox which has to carry a heavy yoke wastes energy carrying the yoke that could more usefully be used to pull the wagon. The cost of a needlessly heavy yoke is obvious, down the road.

Each bit of energy that an ox expends to carry an extra pound of dead yoke weight on its neck keeps it from pulling maybe dozens of extra pounds on a smoothly rolling wagon travelling a straight and narrow path. The teamster knew that pulling the extra weight would slow the ox down so that it covered less distance by the end of the day. An ox with a needlessly heavy yoke would pull thousands of miles less by the end of its working life while costing as much or more as the ox with a lighter yoke.

Excess load makes a badly fitting yoke do more damage to the ox's hooves, shoes, muscles and skeleton, and shortens its working life.

Light is Balance

A light load can be excessive if it is not balanced or loaded properly. A wagon with too much weight over one wheel is more likely to wreck, turn over, or break down. An unbalanced load will tend to do damage. We can do more if we are well-balanced.

An over-the-road trucker today knows all this that his teamster predecessor knew millennia ago. He just doesn't realize that it's in the Bible. Translations that use outmoded technology make it hard for many moderns to understand how brilliant the Author is to have chosen the words He did.

Another thing makes it difficult for moderns: Many have been too dumbed down by Public Education to make the transition between "My yoke is easy, my burden light." and "If I reduce dead weight, I make more money." Lack of up-to-date translations is not the only reason people don't understand the Bible. Thanks to Public Education, many of us can't read as well as our ancestors.

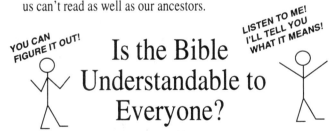

YOU CAN FIGURE IT OUT!

LISTEN TO ME! I'LL TELL YOU WHAT IT MEANS!

Is the Bible Understandable to Everyone?

The very same people have had different answers to that question. Martin Luther began by answering "Yes!". After his new version of the Church on Earth was established, people started to disagree with it. Many didn't go along with his interpretations of the Bible. After a few pesky people questioned him, Luther changed his answer to "No!"

Fundamentalism Affirmed by Current Technology Translation?

The Author did not just foretell the meanings of words that we would use. His power is so awesome that He planned both words and meanings for all times. Since it was words with which He said "Not a sparrow falls without His knowing." He said on a most literal and fundamental level of a Current Technology Translation that the word "sparrow" will not change without His knowing.

"In the Beginning was the Word". Things as complicated as living, breathing animals are just words (Replicating Fractal Formulae) to the God Who made them. He was kind enough to let Adam have the enjoyment of picking words that fit his vastly more limited cerebral apparatus.

Don't Stop With "My Yoke is Easy"

Say, "My power transfer device is infinitely adjustable, perfectly efficient, and easy to move around." Then a modern disciple with engineering skills would immediately understand that Jesus was interested in the elegance of simplicity.

An engineer could calculate just how much pulling efficiency and carrying capacity would be gained by reducing the dead weight of a heavy wooden yoke. He could even graph it. Or, come up with a Rule of Thumb: "For every ounce that the yoke is reduced, an ox can pull two more pounds."

On a straight and narrow path like a runway, a yoke as light as a cotton vest could pull more weight longer and faster than a hundred pound oak yoke. And, as we race down the runway of life, trying to get the load up to enough speed (grace) for takeoff (Heaven admission) who'd be crazy enough to want to carry a heavier-than-necessary yoke?

So, Christ's concern for the yoke demands that we have a concern for the road. Straight, narrow paths (monasteries and convents?) waste the least amount of energy and provide for the greatest efficiency in allowing each of us to move as much as possible during our working years.

There's Always a Yoke on Us

None of us are perfectly made for the work we do. So, we make lots of power transfer devices for ourselves and each other: yokes. We are yoked to cash registers, which allow us to move money around. We are yoked to keyboards and computers to move information around. We yoke ourselves to trucks and wheelbarrows to help us move materials. Pots and pans allow us to move heat to food. Our civilization has thousands of gizmos that we use to transfer people-power to a task. The yokes we make for ourselves and each other are rarely "easy", no matter how "ergonomic" we think them to be. Earthly jobs are rarely tailor-made to fit us and the changing loads we carry without forcing us to utilize power-transfer devices. That's why jobs are called "work".

We are Always Yoked to Yokes. The one thing to which we are always yoked is the need to use yokes. Consider the changes in workload as a child moves through the grades, through the schools, through relocations, through the work force, through marriage and family, through retirement. Jesus says to both Iron and Information Agers with total confidence: "My power transfer device adapts itself perfectly to immense changes in burden, roadway, and speed." The simple translation "My yoke is easy" meant all those things to a prior generation whose society depended upon transferring power from oxen as much as ours depends on transferring energy from fossil and nuclear fuels.

Yokes Imply Training; Training, Discipline. Stubborn people and animals in their natural state resist being yoked. They have to be trained, often from youth, to pull a load. They are born yoked only to instincts, but learn as they grow. Even a cow in a herd of wild cattle picks up a crude discipline. Each will run in the same direction when an enemy approaches. They follow a leader. Letting themselves be yoked to a more intelligent being lets them participate in things far more intelligent than they could think of doing on their own in the wild. The more intelligent the being to whom they are yoked, the more they can get done.

Training implies continuity, systems, and stability. Young, inexperienced animals are often yoked to older, trained animals. This way, the trained animal directly passes on to the trainee the right way to behave. Just as the yoke is a link between the power source and the job, the Training Animal is a living yoke, a link between the trainer and the untrained beast. Just as the new convert is encouraged to walk alongside an experienced Sponsor to learn about his Faith, the inexperienced mule more quickly learns to pull a plow if it is yoked alongside a mule that's broken to harness.

The difference between some men and all mules? An untrained mule has to be roped and dragged to the yoke. He has to be starved, forced, cajoled, or beaten into getting used to it. Many men will get so tired of wandering around in the fields, wearing themselves out accomplishing nothing, that they will show up at the hitching post just hoping someone will put a yoke on them.

Please, Yoke Me!

We often see people drawing attention to themselves. Many of them secretly hope that someone will yoke them and train them to do something useful. They want to be a part of something bigger. They want to do more than they can get done on their own. We can get bitten, kicked, and scratched trying to break wild animals to the yoke. We can have all that done to us, plus being mocked, maligned, and insulted trying to tell wild people about the strange yoke we know about that hitches us to God.

It's important to tell people about The Yoke. We mustn't be too busy to do that. Most of us are so short-sighted that we will spend more time for earthly gain than for Heavenly profit. "If I break the wild oxen, I can plow the field. Then, I can plant, harvest, sell the grain and make more money." is a lot more common concern than "I care so much for heavenly profit that I'll try to get the person who's left spouse and children to be more concerned with God and family than with sin and distractions."

The More We Wear the Yoke, the More We Do With it

Those of us who willingly wear a better yoke improve the quality and quantity of the work we do. We put it on more quickly in the morning, and don't take it off as much during the day. We even wear it home from work. We go to sleep wearing it. St. Augustine said that some of our dreams indicate we don't wear it when we're sleeping, so we know that we can yoke our spirits better while we're awake than while we're asleep.

When people who want to be productive see the results of discipline, their desire for more discipline increases so that they can do more.

Once we see how much more we get done with the yoke, we have less and less desire to take it off. We want to stay on a straight and narrow road that lets us move our load to where we want to go.

Education Exists to Provide Yokes for Brain Cells

Education provides us with yokes to do work in many areas. Learning math yokes our mind to numbers that let us count, weigh, measure, and calculate. Language yokes our mind to ways to communicate. Science lets us yoke our mind to the physical world. Churches want people to learn to yoke themselves to God. Evil people want the minds of children to be yoked to drugs, or to illicit sexual gratification.

Before we put educational yokes on our mind, we should try on the yoke He has for us. It's the only one that claims to be custom made. When all the other yoke-attachments like math and science are attached to it, they work better. There are Christian mathematicians, like Pascal. There are Christian scientists, like Mendel. There are Christian writers, like James Fenimore Cooper. There are Christian parents. You know some.

No yoke that we wear will get anything done just by being worn. Any yoke has to be attached to something if it's going to help do work. Just so with mental yokes. For us to do the highest good at what we do, we have to do it as a believer in God and His Goodness. So, when we learn math, we don't want to use it to calculate the profit we could gain by dealing drugs. We want to find out something useful, how to make or do something that benefits.

So, We Might as Well Get the Best

It is incredible just to know that one has, or can get, or even has been promised, a perfectly fitting and infinitely adjusting power transfer device. The person who has promised us that this marvelous thing exists, and that we can each have one, has been called "Son of God" by people so smart they can reason like St. Aquinas and persuade like St. Augustine. The people who call the Man With the

Perfect Power Transfer Device the "Son of God" are so honest that they believe despite suffering like St. Thomas More and St. Mary. There are good reasons to take the words of good people seriously.

Only One Yoke

He didn't say "My yokes are light . . ." That indicates He has only one yoke for us, and that yoke is His. It indicates that there is no better yoke, and no yoke that is its equal. So, we cannot find a yoke as good as His, or a yoke that is better than His. If we want the best, the choice is clear. He is the best yoke-maker.

Get Beyond the Physical by Understanding the Physical

An implied meaning to be considered: Since the yoke is what allows work to be done, and since a thing that is ultimately "light" doesn't weigh anything at all, Jesus may be saying that "I only have to be, and my work is done. You only have to be one with me, and your work is done."

A message that comes plainly through Aquinas says that God is one. His knowing and His willing are one. If

Aquinas is right, God's Power Source and Transmission could then also be assumed to be one. "My yoke is light." would then also mean, "My power and its transmission are one, and both are made out of light." John says, "In the beginning was the Word, and the Word was light." And, Scripture says He is "the Light of the World". And, with that light, we can begin to see that God could have programmed the Whole Blooming Creation out of multi-dimensional fractals in a few days.

Multi-Dimensional Fractals: Building Blocks of Creation

Most moderns have seen fractal patterns in pictures and in everyday shapes. Some have watched fractal patterns blossom into complicated, organized shapes on TV and computer screens.

It's easy for moderns to take the step from "With fractal geometry, I can program two dimensional formulas that grow and spread beautiful drawings on my computer screen." to "God is much smarter than I am. He can program three dimensional shapes that spread actual structures throughout actual space."

The amazing thing is that people could literally believe in the Bible before they had computers to show them how easy it would have been for God to crank everything out in a week.

Applying fractal geometry to Current Technology Translation opens up whole new avenues for people who don't know what Iron Age implements are. But, Current Technology Translations go two ways. We in the Information Age need Current Technology Translations to make Iron Age implements comparable to their more complicated equivalents. At the other end of human technology, Stone Age tribesmen in the rainforest may need Current Technology Translations with reduced complexity. "My tump line doesn't cause headaches."

What Does "my" Mean?

It might be "The yoke that I have ('my yoke') is both powerful and easy (for you) to move around." or, "The yoke that I am putting on you, or providing you who choose to put it on, is a power-transfer device that is both powerful and easy to move around." "My car is easy to drive, so take it for a spin."

"My" also implies that He shares in the work He makes available for us, as with a double yoke. "Step up into the empty slot in my yoke. I'll be right next to you, helping you pull your load. I'll be showing you how, every step we take. That way, you know that the burden won't have too much drag for us to overcome."

Yoke Implies Hierarchy

"Yoke" can also be taken as a verb that means "harnessing the power of others." This implies a hierarchy of being. Harnesser and harnessee. Men are allowed to utilize the output of lesser beasts. They are also allowed to utilize the output of lower-ranking people. Some people, like some animals, resist being yoked. Animals run away and sulk. People do the same thing. Some become leftists.

In a possibility thoroughly unpopular with many moderns, He may be saying "I am giving you (The faithful priesthood from Melchizedek on, and/or all the believers since Abel) a yoke that will allow you to obtain sustenance from people still mired in working with the things of Creation.

There are times when each of us is allowed to tell others what to do. When we tell the waitress what we want, we are harnessing cook, busboy, cashier; everybody in the restaurant.

Yokes Increase Output, Increased Output Can Be Measured

When a yoke is put on us, or we yoke someone or some animal, harnessing takes place. As soon as that happens, the being that is harnessed can be judged on output in two ways: 1. What is its output? 2. What percentage of the theoretical maximum output was reached? A formula derived from those and other figures (hopefully including handicaps!) may determine the place in eternity of each yoke-wearer.

There may be a Heavenly Scorecard like "John Smith had the physical, mental, and financial resources to bring five children into the world, but he only had one. At Soul-Production, he only gets 20%, but liberals had convinced him that overpopulation was a real problem. He was too dumbed-down by Public Education to realize that liberals always lie. That gives him a handicap of 60, so he scores 80 and gets ten years in Purgatory starting on Level 9."

On a scarier note, Adam and Eve were thrown out of the Garden for eating one apple.

Each productive sector of our lives is measured some-how. Current Technology Translation gives us an idea of ways to look at Final Scores.

Return on Investment is a method that a Current Technology Translation brings to a discussion of Final Judgment. This is a particularly frightening notion, but one that has to be considered by everyone who wants a broad overview of how he or she may fare when the Chairman of the Board has the President tell the controller who's getting a pension when the factory closes down.

The faithful have invested a considerable amount in the production and maintenance of each soul. If our parents were believers, they fed us, housed us, educated us, and acquainted us with the basics of the faith. We were encouraged in every good thing we did by people who loved us and invested time and energy in us. They took us fishing and to ball games. They took us to school and to Church. To the doctor. They gave counsel and advice. They kept us from harm. They prayed for us.

In today's dollars, measuring only time and energy that family members spent on us, we may have had millions invested into our spiritual account, all with the unspoken aim of having us first save our own souls and then produce and/or save as many other souls as possible.

Other investments were made on our behalf in blood. Prophets let themselves be tortured and killed for us. Jesus, too. Saints and martyrs suffered and shed blood for us. So did many veterans.

If we do not provide those who invested in us with a return on investment, like any non-producing assets, we may be sold at a bankruptcy auction.

Current Technology Translation Suggests Purpose of Free Markets

Among the most important things a Free Market does: provide us with a guideline of how many souls we should be saving. A business that increases its assets at ten percent a year will double about every seven years.

If we live seventy years, and if the The Chairman is only as demanding an an average CEO, for what will we be held accountable? If we are expected to start saving souls when we're fourteen, we should have saved our own by then.

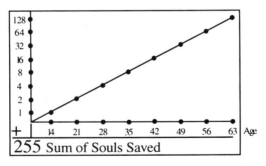

On a straight, ascending asset-accumulation line, in the seven years between the ages of fourteen and twenty one, we should have saved two. Between then and age twenty eight, we should save four. By thirty five, eight. By forty two, sixteen. By forty nine, thirty two. By fifty six, we should have saved sixty four souls. If we can afford to retire from this most important work by sixty three, we will have saved two hundred fifty five souls. We can stop there if we think that the words "Well done, thou good and faithful servant!" will be spoken to a professional worker in the vineyard who only performs as well as an average executive in a Free Market.

Free Markets Provide Opportunities to Exercise Free Will

Re: Saving our own souls. Working in a free market exposes us to all the temptation we need to test our resistance. A man who'll lie for a dollar short-circuits himself so badly he'll have a hard time getting into a place where he can lie for millions. A man in a position to lie for a million, however, may have built up enough momentum to keep himself in a position where he can keep right on lying for a long time.

Every single day in a free market, we each have lots of opportunities to lie, to cheat, and to steal. Each day, we are given the opportunity to commit lots of sins. Freely choosing to do what is right in each of those situations helps us save our own souls.

Re: Saving the souls of others. Often, we do not save souls by simply talking to them. Some people who have moved/been moved closer to God are saved when someone like Billy Graham says: "Believe in God and accept Jesus as your saviour. Do it right now because you may die very soon."

Most are not able to respond quickly to something so utterly true. They may be saved after thinking about the examples that other people have set. We can help to save the souls of others by always being truthful. The Free Market gives us lots of ways to show that we can rise above temptation.

Often, we do not know what a positive influence we have on others by being strong enough to avoid the sins they know that we can commit.

Free Market Yokes Are Voluntary. Government Yokes Aren't.

Taxation is a crushing yoke. It is always heavier than it needs to be. The heavy yoke of taxation can only be put on by raw power. So, Governments and their employees spend a lot of time getting power over people.

The things that Americans can be taxed to pay for were

expressly limited by the U.S. Constitution. The Constitution was written to limit Government, which does not like to be limited.

Many people want Government Jobs because they pay well, don't usually require a lot of work, have very little stress, and great benefits. They want Government to use its taxing power to get money from their neighbors and give it to them. In and of itself, this is not thought to be criminal, especially since it is the Government that makes the laws. It becomes a Serious Commandment Violation when a bureaucrat takes money from taxpayers and doesn't do anything useful with it.

A bureaucrat who abuses his power to take without giving as much or more than he takes is stealing. Each theft of taxpayer money is compounded by a lie. "We did good and useful things for you with the money we took from you." says every government agency through its myriads of PR people.

What did Jesus think of that when the Romans were doing it? Not much. "Give those who worship the things of Creation what they want of those things." He didn't think much of liars and thieves who gorged on tax money. And, He didn't see much need for excessively complaining about people who lie to steal tax money. He didn't seem to think much of things. He, better than anyone, knew that the things people bought with the money were only stage props.

The message He is giving us? Creation exists to see who wants parts of it more than they want to know the Creator.

Still, Believers Hate to See Tax Money Wasted

When Believers pay taxes, many of them agonize. "They are taking money away from me and my family. They are wasting it on insane programs that have no hope of working. They are stealing from me and lying to justify it. On top of that, the poor bureaucrats may be going to Hell because they are so addicted to the things of Creation and I can't see any way to tell them what's going to happen to them."

It is very hard to convert tyrants, especially the petty ones usually selected to staff government offices where taxpayers can be told "No." Petty tyrants are frightened people. Those who work on useless tax-supported jobs end up being twisted by the Government Yoke.

The Government Yoke is only rarely attached to a real load. In the private sector, workers provide goods and services that people freely choose to procure. Private sector people have to provide satisfaction. People in useless agencies only have to lie to get more money. So, their yoke isn't attached to a balanced load. It's attached to lies and deception. Lies and deceptions are not stable loads. They're always shifting around and are hard to pull. Pulling a load of lies burns people out.

Sometimes, the yoke worn by government employees in useless jobs is attached to a pole, which only allows those connected to it to go around and around. They are not happy people, but they console themselves by promising: "As soon as I retire, what I want to do is. . ." Whatever their plans, what they want to do is go straight.

If we wear Jesus' yoke, we get to do that as soon as we put it on. When we carry a load, and go straight, we get straightened out.

Yokes Don't Work Alone

Yokes are Hitched to a shaft or some other sort of connector. A yoke does not work alone. It may have many attachments between the work and the worker. A yoke necessitates more post-yoke power transfer devices.

Then, Comes the Whole World. A yoke is attached to a shaft which is attached to a drawbar attached to swivel pins attached to an axle. The axle is removably attached on its ends to hubs, from which spokes radiate. Wheels are formed by carefully carved fellows and covered with rims. On top, the axle is fastened to springs which are attached to the wagon bed. The axle may be attached at the back to another axle. There are bolts, pegs, hames, reins, rims, whips, goads, grease, gates, brakes, brackets, buckets, buckles, beds, covers, hoops, sides, sleeves, springs, spokes, seats, swivels, straps, and on and on and on.

Each of these things is indirectly connected to the yoke. Each of these things helps transfer power from the source to the job.

The yoke necessitated the development of these auxiliary power transfer devices. Yokes caused the technologies in metallurgy, mining, mathematics, and every other field that made them possible. The yoke was the key that opened the door to the building of roads, the digging of ditches, and the installation of culverts. Inns, armored chariots, taxing authorities, and all the other accoutrement of modern, specialized society are connected to the yoke.

For Him to say His yoke is better than every single component of every single society that is connected to and moved by the power transfer devices of its age is saying something incredibly powerful. Only a Current Technology Translation helps us to see it.

Because the man who invented the yoke did not hide his light under a bushel, he made all the other things possible, along with all the jobs of all the makers of all the other things. The proportion of inventors to others may be about the same as the proportion of yeast to dough.

Yoked to Honest Work

There are two kinds of work: 1. Free Market Work, which is freely entered into, as when we hire a local carpenter to remodel our kitchen. 2. Forced work, as when we're made to pay school administrators' lush salaries while our own income goes down as fast as our childrens' reading ability.

When we don't do an honest day's work for an honest day's pay, we are very, very unhappy. We know that other people have given us money, and we know that we are wasting it. When we do that, our actions tell the people whose money it is that we despise them and what they do for a living. If we despise our neighbors, we despise ourselves.

And, we don't enjoy despising ourselves for a living.

The best kind of work has two components:

1. It is work that we choose to do.
2. It is work for which we are paid because people freely chose <u>us</u> to do the work.

Work that has those two components is satisfying. It is work of which we can be proud. When we can say: "People with free will in a free market freely chose ME as the source of their goods or services." we are saying something that few bureaucrats can ever say.

We may not have the stultifying steady income, and the mind-numbing automatic raises that bureaucrats get, but we're in a different class. We don't want things that can destroy our minds and souls. Free market people are often of a higher class. So are useful bureaucrats. We have the deep, abiding enjoyment of satisfying ourselves by satisfying other people.

We must pity the poor, overpaid bureaucrats in useless agencies who go through life squeezing people to get their money. They have less job satisfaction than ditchdiggers. Some of them are driven to drugs, sexual perversion, eating disorders, arrogance, withdrawal, depression and all the other manifestations of wasted, unfulfilled abilities.

The hardest work that bureaucrats in the useless agencies have to do is to pretend that they are doing something useful. That is the most exhausting work of all. They are yoked to lunacy. They are driven around in circles, raising huge clouds of dust and getting nowhere.

They are yoked to lies, then to theft. Then, armed robbery and murder. Still, they do have free will. They can get useful jobs in useful places.

The Most Important Early Lesson of the Yoke

Men saw that where there was power, that it was possible to harness that power. No longer were powerful bulls in the Bronze Age simply something to be eaten, sacrificed, or played with in arenas by acrobats. The yoke made bulls useful beyond the brief period of time they were used for food, skin, or stud.

The bull is made of light. The sun was made and caused grass to grow. The bull ate the grass. Putting a yoke on a bull is putting a yoke on the light it absorbed. Current Technology Translation lets us see that yoking the bull is using God's power to help us.

With a yoke, men could harness the bull to cut grass and drag it into barns. There, the sunlight stored in dead grass gave the bull strength throughout the winter to pull wagons and drag logs to build bigger barns to hold more sunlight stored in bigger haystacks.

When men learned that they could yoke bulls, it was a short step for them to harness other forms of power that came from light, like rivers and wind.

If We're Tired? Weary?

To Get Beyond the Physical Nature of the Yoke we can consider the words that He chose to precede the passage at hand. "Come to me all you who are weary and heavily burdened (with life), and I will refresh you. Take my yoke upon your shoulders and learn from me, for I am gentle and humble of heart. Your soul will find rest." Then, "My yoke is easy and my burden is light" concludes the passage.

So, if we are weary, and find life too heavy, we're invited to carry our load with the spiritual mechanisms He uses and makes available. We get weary not because the burden is too heavy, but because we aren't handling it properly. That happens when we aren't pulling our weight correctly. The mechanisms we are using to move our life from and through stage to stage just don't work.

Life may be chafing us, rubbing us raw. If our problems are truly hurting us, the burdens of life may be actually driving us crazy. We have to get tired of this kind of suffering, rather than just getting used to it, or, worse yet, actually liking it.

Seeing that we do not have to suffer needlessly is often the first step to getting the best yoke.

Bad Yokes

There are many ways that a yoke won't fit. Each type of misfitted yoke causes a different injury. A minor imperfection on the surface of the yoke causes callous. A badly warped yoke causes the ox to pull out of line. Pulling from the wrong angle will twist and damage its spine.

Growing up, some people have to carry loads that twist them. Abusive, overpowering parents. Abusive, overpowering governments.

In life, the different manifestations of a badly fitting yoke are obvious. Obese people manifest one type of misfitting yoke. Sexually perverted people have another. Alcoholics and drug addicts have similar types of yoke misfittedness, different than angry people.

Sometimes, we can see that something is wrong with a person just by seeing how he carries himself.

Often, an ox gets so used to a badly fitting yoke that it fights getting into a properly fitting one. "Come, on, Babe," the farmer cajoles, "this one is lots better for you, even if it does hurt, now." If the ox could talk, it may say: "But, I've gotten used to this yoke. It will hurt to reform muscles and cartilage into new shapes, even if it is better for me."

No matter how used we get to the adjustments we've made to pull our load through life, remedial yokes are needed, slowly forcing the deformed body back into proper alignment.

That's why Jesus says: "Take my yoke upon your shoulders and learn from me."

Once we get that yoke on, we get straightened out. In fact, the load we pull helps to straighten us out. The harder we work with His yoke, the better we become. There are no efficiency-robbing angles between us and the load, nothing exists that can come between us and the most efficient use of our abilities.

Magic Hidden in This Passage

"Take my yoke upon your shoulders." The magic: He doesn't tell us to take our old, badly fitting yoke off. When we put His on, our old, bent, twisted, splintered yoke just goes away. Even if the yoke we used to wear was made for us by the Devil, himself, and we sold our soul to get it, all we have to do is pick up the yoke Jesus has for us.

His yoke gently and slowly corrects our faults. Impatience becomes patience. Rage, joy. Not that very minute. It can take years to get straightened out. It's like braces, on teeth. Slow and steady does it every time. When we put His yoke on, life gets easier. And, the view gets better. Because we see the light, we avoid potholes and pitfalls. We cover more ground with less work.

Yoke as Rest?

When we consider this promise, "Your soul will find rest", we can conclude that the soul is something that can be in a state of unrest. The relief He promises is not from just the load we carry, but also from unrest we feel about carrying the wrong load, or from carrying the right load improperly.

So, what is a soul? What is this thing which, when it does not live in rest, makes us weary and causes us to see life as a burden?

Start with what the soul isn't. It isn't our body, or He would have said "Your body will find rest." It isn't our mind, or He would have said "Your mind will find rest." Elsewhere, Scripture says that the soul is different from the spirit.

The passages say that the soul is something that can be wearied and discouraged. Therefore, it also can be energized and enthusiastic. The passage says that the soul can be refreshed, which means that it must be something that can go stale.

Jesus says that the soul responds positively to gentleness from a humble heart. His words imply that the soul cringes from harshness swelling out of vanity and conceit. The soul is something that can find rest, so it is something that can get tired. All of these things indicate that the soul responds to, and is heavily influenced by, feelings that come from outside itself.

The soul must be a life-form so subtle that it can feel oppressed simply by perceiving arrogance and vanity. Gloriously relieved by finding truth.

Compare it to a sunflower which moves to follow an obvious source of light.

It sounds very much as if the soul is the joy of feeling synchronization. But, it may be more inclusive than that. It may not be just 'a feeling', but just plain feeling. Consider an ordinary conversation, "By the size of that cast it looks like you broke your leg. How do you feel?" *"Wonderful! How about you?"* "That's amazing. You feel fine, on crutches with your leg in a cast?" *"My wife just had a baby."* "That explains it. Congratulations!"

From our own experience, do we try to tell the state of other souls by asking how they feel? Can they can tell something about our souls, too?

Yoke as Love

When we can love our neighbor as ourselves, we can stop envying, disliking, and looking down on our neighbor. When we can do that, we swim in a perfect sea. We become fish in a synchronized school, birds in a synchronized flock, completely individual while at one with a greater whole.

And, we can avoid disparaging what honest work our neighbor does with the yoke he has freely chosen to put on. One conclusion is that His yoke is love, and the shaft that connects that yoke to the load is forgiveness.

"Take My Yoke Upon Your Shoulders and Learn From Me"

We cannot learn without words. If we are to learn from Him, then the yoke is more than literal. Somehow, the yoke has to be able to talk, to give us words. We are supposed to take His yoke literally on our shoulders, like a gardener puts on a wooden shoulder yoke for carrying water buckets. But, we are to realize that it is not just a thing of wood we carry, but a thing of words.

Does the yoke prefigure the cross? Is the sacrifice of ourselves what we must ultimately carry? Is the yoke putting others ahead of ourselves? Giving of ourselves to others? Letting ourselves work more efficiently to serve others? Do we use the yoke to carry God's Word to those who do not have it?

The ox does not begin by knowing that it was brought into being to pull. The ox may never know that it was bred and born to simply pull. No matter how it resists, it is trained, long and arduously, to pull. It will do that, or be eaten. Making the ox pull is what its master feels will provide Him the most profit.

The yoke only helps him pull better. The first yoke was probably a rope tied around the ox's neck. It was a failure. It choked him to death if he tried to pull something. The better the yoke, the more the ox could do without hurting itself. Wearing a good yoke of a good master lets the puller do more without hurting himself.

We Actually Can Put His Yoke Physically On

One way that some people put on His yoke is to try to imitate Him in every way. He was generous, so they become generous. He was honest, so they never tell lies. He would rather help others than make himself rich, they do the same.

This can be a dead-end road. Without the Sacraments and the Church for guidance, it is very easy for such people to go astray. When successful, they say "See what I can do? I can get to Heaven on my own." An overly individual effort can turn into a one-person Tower of Babel.

Some who try a do-it-yourself ascent to Heaven end up believing that the Government provides useful outlets for idealists. These foolish innocents think that the Peace Corps is different from the CIA.

Most of the time, an individual who sincerely tries to imitate Christ will see a lack of direction, and be drawn to the Church.

Each Ox has its own Yoke

The souls of men are worth more than an ox. But, even an ox can have a yoke custom-trimmed and finished to fit it. Since we are vastly more important than an ox, each of us has our own custom-made yoke for the job we're meant to do. Some yokes are bigger than others so that we each do different amounts of the same job. Some yokes are worn longer than others. There's an amount of work that we can do, and the amount of work that we end up doing. The closer the second amount comes to the first, the closer to sainthood we get.

"Take My Yoke Upon Your Shoulders and Learn From Me, For I am Gentle and Humble of Heart."

Before we take the yoke, the first thing we have to do is to choose to take His yoke upon our shoulders. If we don't do that, we can't learn from Him. There is an indication of free will, an implied choice. He does not give the imperious command He has every right to give: "I am the Son of God. You *must* take my yoke. . ." There is only a simple suggestion, "Take my yoke . . ." If force or coercion were implied, He would not have finished by telling us that He was gentle and humble in his innermost being.

We do not even have to choose to immediately pick up His yoke to begin. "Take" has more than one meaning. It means to physically get ahold of, but it also means to examine closely. We are being told what we should tell potential believers: "Take a look at that." "Please, take this under consideration."

A gentle, humble heart would not abruptly order us to choose to physically pick up something and carry it before giving us a long, long opportunity to examine it carefully from all angles.

It's Nice, Having an Infinitely Variable Transmission

Knowing that we have to carry our lives along with us helps us to focus more clearly upon what our work is. Focus cuts down on distractions. We stop worrying about speed. Sometimes, we have to go very slowly. We speak very slowly to children about complicated things. And, to older people. Other times, we have to go fast. We have jobs to do so well that we get promoted instead of fired.

Each of our tasks requires a different approach, a varied speed, a new way of thinking about things. The new, promised yoke will allow us to work through these problems, and many more besides. If the teachings of the Saints are even close to right, we will never have a problem we can't pull our way through if we have the Right Yoke.

Speaking of Pulling

A yoke isn't made for pushing. It's made for pulling. That tells us something very profound. Think of the difference between pushing and pulling. First, when we're pushing, we can't always see where we're going. Pushing compresses our joints and causes arthritis. Pushing is a brute force action that we're always forced to do when something complicated breaks.

Over the long haul, we call a tow truck to pull, not a

shove truck to push. A primitive farmer pushing a plow can barely feed his family. A farmer pulling a huge plow behind a huge tractor can feed a town. We should only push brooms.

Pulling is Pushing is Pulling

Pushing and pulling are related. The ox pushes its hooves against the ground to shove itself forward. Four separate shoves, one leg at a time, complete a cycle that can be repeated and turned into a steady pull. Each separate downward push of each leg is followed by an upward pull. Complicated strands of muscle propel each stroke.

Each strand of muscle can only pull. The pulling of thousands of individual strands of muscle pushes the animal against the yoke. The yoke, in turn, becomes a mechanism for pulling.

Pushing and shoving is for people or occupations that haven't advanced to yokes. Pushing doesn't have as many sophisticated kinds of power transfer devices. People who are "pushy" don't get as far as people with "pull".

When we push something, its front end digs into the ground, and it's almost impossible to move. When we pull an object, we tend to raise its front end. That minimizes friction and takes vastly less effort to move. The yoke tends to lift the shaft, and the wagon is pulled forward while its front end is lifted slightly upwards. That lets it roll more easily over irregularities in the road.

Bulldozers push and shove. But, they tear up the roads, too, unless they're pulled from place to place on trailers yoked to tractors.

Some Don't get the Yoke

In the earliest days of the Iron Age, only the rich and successful had yokes. Adam and Eve used to look at Cain and shake their heads. "Poor kid. He can't figure out how to yoke the cattle. Must take after your side of the family." Cain was always steaming. Not only did he not have a yoke that fit, he didn't even have a yoke at all.

For years, people without yokes were looked down on, treated as second class citizens. Settlers who could yoke animals were always wiping out native people who couldn't. Yokeless people just don't get as much done.

"And, after God spent all that time making cattle for us.", snobbish yoke-owners would sniff in disdain. Cain got mad about it. Abel probably had a yoke. Maybe, Abel invented the yoke. Abel was a lot smarter than Cain. Didn't Cain hate that? When we have the right yoke, we can be happy carrying our own load without being jealous of people with different loads.

And, God didn't destroy Cain for killing Abel. Actually, God protected Cain, and wouldn't let anyone else destroy Cain, either. Abel may have deserved what he got.

Abel May Have Thought He Was Real Smart

Maybe, Abel made the mistake a lot of smart people make: He took personal credit for being smart. "Look at me, I'm so smart! My sacrifice is lots better than *yours!*"

We all know insufferable people. People who are truly smart know the most important things about intelligence:

1. Obedience counts for lots more than intelligence to the Vastly Smarter mind of God. He Who is Infinitely Smarter than the smartest of us knows that we're all dumb, compared to Him.

2. No one makes himself smart. A person can no more take credit for being smart than for being seven or eight feet tall.

3. It's nice to be smart, but Hell is crammed with people who thought that being Real Smart was all there is to it.

4. Ordinary people learn that 1, 2, and 3 are true long before smart people.

So, Where do we go From Here?

We need to go to a new Translation of the Bible, if only in our minds. We don't need the silly translations we've been getting lately, like the New Translations To Make Women Feel Good. In them, God the Father becomes a Parent Almighty, at best, or Goddess The Mother, in the more extreme translations. Others are designed to make other special interests look good. They read accordingly, and we can see through them easily.

Martin Luther made one of the very first Political Translations. He left out the parts of the Old Testament that concerned praying for the dead, because his political bosses didn't want folks giving money to the Church when they could pay taxes with it, instead. He tried to leave out the Book of James, because of that inconvenient bit about "Faith without works is dead."

When we read Bible translations, we're often seeing agendas. Is there an agenda in this espousal of a Current Technology Translation? Yep. People should all have an opportunity to be saved and have at least an indication that their Government can't do it for them. When we look at the Bible and see familiar things, we can relate to God's Word as well as did the Iron Age farmers in Sussex working Lord Muckamuck's land in 1214.

What follows is NOT a complete translation. Just a new way to think about reading and translating, if only in our minds, a small part of Holy Scripture. If we learn to translate things in our minds, and force ourselves to see the modern counterparts of Iron-Age language, we may see things we've missed. We may be able to tell other people about the Most Unusual Man with the infinitely variable transmission that's made out of light.

A Most Amazing Thing We May Learn is about how His Father could have used mathematical formulas somewhat more complicated than our own Fractal Geometry to program actual 3-D shapes with which sub-programmers could have made all Creation in only seven days.

Old Testament
Current Technology
Translations:

If the Genesis Account of Creation is literally correct, the world was made in precisely seven days, each of which had twenty-four hours.

Most moderns are trained to automatically dismiss that. We just can't see how something that simplistic could be correct. We recoil from the notion with jerk-knee speed.

Microscopes and telescopes continually reveal things that make Creation seem more complicated. New discoveries make it especially unbelievable that He could have made everything in Seven Days. Many believers waffle. They try to believe and still give credit to the science/government establishment. They say: "Well, we don't know how long a day was, back then."

Fundamentalists with more faith rise above this hoary cop-out, but they still can't make their beliefs seem very realistic. Today, a Current Technology Translation shows that Fundamentalism is far more feasible than science. Why? Current Technology makes the traditional beliefs more believable than they have ever been.

Today, a tiny handful of believers have a chance to evangelize the world by showing how the latest technology validates the faith of our fathers.

Beyond Your
Computer to
Shapes in Space

When using the computer, we see images on the screen. The shapes have length and width, two dimensions. God, Who's vastly smarter, can do this in more dimensions.

When God "prints out", He can "print out" multi-dimensional shapes.

Compare how smart we are.
We can take a shape like this:
and turn it into infinity.

We see it every time we turn on a calculator.

can be used to make   and   and

all the other numbers, up to

and beyond.

If God is only as much smarter than we are as it is possible for us to imagine,

He can do more than turn   into

He can turn this   into

In space. No screen. No paper.
Just shapes in space.

The Fractal Theory of Creation

Imagine that you have programmed your computer to draw an inch long section of a garden hose, a simple section of a tube. Then, with a crude program, you tell the computer to draw other sections the same size right next to it. If you could set your print command to "Infinite Repeat", you could imagine printing out an endless line of tubes next to each other.

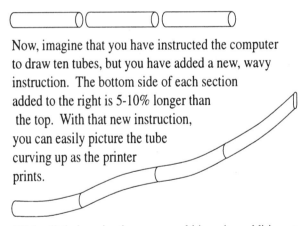

Now, imagine that you have instructed the computer to draw ten tubes, but you have added a new, wavy instruction. The bottom side of each section added to the right is 5-10% longer than the top. With that new instruction, you can easily picture the tube curving up as the printer prints.

With a little imagination, you could imagine additions to the program that would cause the tube to split, and the new branches, with slight changes in the program, could spiral off in different directions.

Then, picture your printer drawing something like a simple plant, growing two branches, one on the right circling up and to the right, the one on the left circling up and to the left. You could learn to program your computer to draw pictures. You could even have your computer draw vastly more complicated shapes.

Men do this every day in vastly greater detail with Fractal Geometry. The formulae used in that discipline will draw shapes that grow and replicate in various sizes all over the screen, growing, shrinking, changing colors.

Now, imagine that God had programmed that in three dimensions.

First, He may have programmed a basic shape. Maybe, something like this:

Then, stacked them:

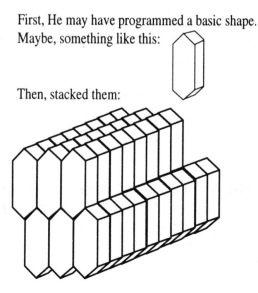

It's possible that He combined
Basic Shape sub-programs
into bigger programs.
For plant design, He may
have had a Stem Program,
including tiny tubes that
could carry droplets from the
Water Program up from below,
where they entered the Root
Program. At the other end,
instructions in the Leaf Program
would cause its chemicals to turn
energy from the Sun and
Light Programs into energy
that would fuel the process.

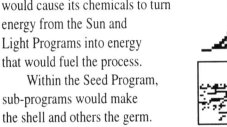

Within the Seed Program,
sub-programs would make
the shell and others the germ.
Within those sub-programs, other sub-programs would
make colors, chemicals,and all the other structures that go
on and on.

The key point: Believing that God can program little
shapes. Put together, those building blocks can make the
sub-atomic particles that make the atoms that make the
elements that make the compounds that make everything

else. A surprisingly few number of shapes are necessary. Even fewer connector shapes are needed.

Not being able to imagine that God is smart enough to program actual shapes that can be put together to make all the things in Creation is what causes all the trouble in the world.

The second we admit to ourselves that God *could* do that much programming, we have taken a big step toward Him.

With a Current Technology Translation, the very first step to belief is a simple First Question:

Is it possible that a being intelligent enough to program actual shapes with actual dimensions exists?

If it appears to be possible, then consider a Statement of Fact and a Second Question:

Statement of Fact: *The owner of a software company can hire many programmers, each one working on separate components of a desired program.*

If we think there is a chance that we are made in the image of God, can we go from the above Statement of Fact to the:

Second Question: *Can God program sub-programmers who can, in turn, program more sub-programmers to program and produce the very building blocks of Creation?*

Anyone who has watched a screen saver spread magically across a screen knows that man can program in two dimensions. Is it reasonable to believe that God can program in multi-dimensions?

To answer "Yes." is to have taken a modern step along an ancient path. That answer can begin to move us into a Unique System that says we have a rightful place in life and we that we have a right to it. We start to fit our own, unique programs into the Big Program. We can move into accepting that the Testaments are true, that The Church is right, that there is a Final Judgment, that we can be saved. We can be happy.

After We Take Those First Steps, we have to do something odd. For a minute, we have to suspend our old logic and stand on sheer belief. Purely human structures of logic did not get people to God at Babel. Human logic alone won't get us to Him, now. First, we must believe. Then, we will understand.

Trying to understand without believing can't get anywhere. It's a programming error on the order of Eating The Apple. It's a First Commandment violation that says "I think I'm more important than God."

Many cannot start out by actually believing. What they may do to test out the benefits of belief is say to themselves: "I am going to think and act as if I believe."

To begin to solve the problems of the world, we must see how we fit into it.

Five Quick Steps to get in Tune with Current Technology Translations:

1. Begin by believing that if there is a God, He is immensely smarter than we are. Repeat this simple, comforting truth to yourself throughout the day, "If God is real, He is immensely smarter than I am."

2. Consciously realize that His programming abilities are vastly ahead of ours. Repeat to yourself: "He can program far, far better than we can."

3. See that He can program in three or more dimensions when He wants. "I can program my computer to draw simple things. He can program me out of the elements and I can program my computer to draw simple things."

4. Understand that He can program tiny structures that can fit into programs of vastly larger structures. Building blocks are made of building blocks.

5. Realize that He can program programmers that can make sub-programmers that can program sub-sub-programmers, and so on. In the Middle Ages, this progression was known as "The Hierarchy Of Angels".

HEY, GOD . . . TWO NICE PROGRAMS!

The Three Kinds of Bible Translations

Until now, most Bible Translations were made to put forward a *linguistic* or a *political* point of view.

The *linguistic* translations are increasingly silly. Most of them are translated by well-intentioned scholars in a rut. They try to make their faith appeal to Information Age people by telling them how Scripture relates to Iron Age cultures.

In a *political* translation, Martin Luther eliminated the Books of the devoutly religious Maccabees. They were a Jewish family who overthrew the established government when it attacked the Jewish faith. Luther's political over-lords didn't want to be overthrown by devout believers. So, they had him come up with reasons to get those Maccabees out of the Bible. Obediently, Luther removed the best example in Scripture of overtaxed workers who successfully took up arms to defend their faith and their freedom from government tyranny.

Many modern Bible Translations are designed to diminish differences that God programmed between races, sexes, species, and individuals. In the new *political* translations, all hierarchies are levelled with imaginary equalities. In those translations, it is nothing less than the programming and judgment of God which is attacked.

When we ask ourselves "Who would attack God?", the answer ought to be obvious.

Historical Constant: all *political* Bible Translations are made to elevate the political, economic, and social status of those who are paying for the Translation.

Anyone who has waded through the endless desexing of new translations knows how obvious their purposes are.

What follows is merely an introduction of a new way to Translate. Not from a *Linguistic* or *Political* Ideology, but from an utterly neutral Current Technology viewpoint. It's a whole new platform on which people in the Information Age can stand and see just how Utterly Superior God is. In words that Techies around the world can understand.

In our age, we see that computers allow us to process massive amounts of information. More importantly, computers allow us to *envision the processing* of vastly more massive amounts of information than we, ourselves, can actually process.

Five thousand years of technical progress has led us from painting animals on cave walls all the way to photographing atoms. Looking at those photographs, we can see how intelligent the Church Fathers were to ask themselves how many angels (sub-programmers) can dance among the caverns, peaks, plateaus, and valleys on the head of a pin whose atomic structure they designed and built.

There are few questions of more importance.

Begin with the Genesis

What follows is a new look at the beginning of Genesis. Most of us are partly familiar with that Book, but this Current Technology Translation is different from the others. It lets us see how a Bible translated for Iron-Agers applies to us.

Since the apple, since the Tower of Babel, since the death of His Son, God has given us free rein of our intellects. Today, as at Babel, the structures that we've built make many of us think we're too smart to need God. Our structures seem so impressive that God disappears in the concrete.

Analyze what follows, a small Current Technology Translation of a small part of Genesis, and you will see a way to help others discover how smart God is and how eternal His Scripture is.

1

In the Beginning, God created the Heavens and the Earth. And the Earth was without form and void. Darkness covered the deep, while His mighty wind swept over the waters.

The Beginning did not begin until God put the Master Program into place. He needed a beginning only because the future Free Will Creatures would not have the ability to make choices without a reality based on a beginning. God could exist in formless void. Man could not.

Then God said, "Let there be light," and there was light. God saw how good the light was. God then separated the light from the darkness. God called the light "day" and the darkness, "night". Evening came; and morning followed—the first day.

When God said "Let there be light.", He wasn't just calling into existence what Iron Age people thought of as 'light'. He was calling into existence all of the wavelengths of the entire energy spectrum. In the Old Translations, the whole of the energy spectrum is called "light", because the wavelengths on either side were invisible and unknown to Technologies Past.

Since this passage about light is the very first "Let there be. . .", we should look at it as the first programming instruction. St. Thomas Aquinas knew more about the nature of God than you or I. His conclusion that God is One must be respected if it cannot be contradicted.

If God is One, when He speaks, He programs. When He programs, He wills. When He wills, He does. His first recorded "Let there be . . ." was energy, the waves from one end of the energy spectrum to the other. The tiny, visible part of the spectrum is so important to the process by which the Free Will Creatures are able to save themselves that when it is missing, its absence causes the non-fractal state of darkness, during which time the Free Will Creatures have a hard time seeing what's going on. Light and Dark alternate, like the on-off of a binary, and form the beginning of all organization. Suddenly, the Void had Form.

A note on programming: With human computers, the binary is either "off" or "on". God's programming ability is not so limited. To start with, He also has the ability to use "switching", so He can program with "off", "on", and "switching". That provides tremendous compactness in His programs. He also has "switching on" and "switching off", which gives Him vastly even more compaction in His programs. Obviously, He has whatever programming abilities He wants.

When God said "Let there be light" what He may also have been saying is "Let there be a sub-programmer (Lucifer?) to program light." Visible sources for the light that give the Free Will Creatures lots of things to think about were yet to be programmed. God may or may not have programmed all the nine orders of angels (programmers, sub-programmers, sub-sub programmers, and so on) for each day's programming. Or, the higher orders of angels came first, with the original programs.

When He said "Let there be light." He was also saying "I will have all the wavelengths of the energy spectrum called 'light' in Iron Age translations of the Bible."
The Free Will Creatures to come had to be able to see some wavelengths with their eyes alone while working through Stone, Bronze, and Iron Age technologies. When appropriate, The Free Will Creatures became aware of the other wavelengths.

Free Will Creatures could see light in two ways: They could see some wavelengths directly, as when they came from the sun or a candle. They could also see light that reflected from things. And, they could distinguish between a few million colors in the tiny part of the energy spectrum that was visible to them. Other wavelengths became apparent to the Free Will Creatures as they discovered new energy absorption and measuring devices.

It is possible that He made only some parts of the spectrum at that time. For example, the radio wavelengths may not have been programmed to appear until just before the Free Will Creatures invented radios. It may have been more economical to program the entire spectrum at once. Would He waste energy?

Then God said, "Let there be a dome in the middle of the waters, to separate the waters." And so it happened. God made the dome, and separated the water above the dome from the water below it. God called the dome "the sky". Evening came, and morning followed—the second day.

The dome, the gasses of the air, was the result of additional basic fractal programs. Each of the components of the atmosphere had to be made for its own sake, as well as for the purposes of the complicated water fractals and all that would depend on the two and their relationships.

According to the very first passages in the Programming Manual, "waters" existed before He recorded the

Programming Process. The dome allowed the cruder, pre-programming "waters" to become one water that could go from solid to liquid to gaseous states depending on the amount of energy absorbed from the light and other fractals.

Today, a Current Technology Translation could call one aspect of the "dome" a "miniscus layer" where "surface tension" divides water in liquid form from water in vapor form. The "dome" not only separates the water in a pond from the air above it, but also keeps the contents of each raindrop inside each raindrop.

This brilliant fractal formula was a syntheses of two vastly more elementary fractal sub-programs, today known as hydrogen and oxygen. The incredible new design that combined them allowed for three or more forms to be manifested from one substance. God had brilliantly invented particles that could tirelessly change back and forth from solid to liquid to gas. The water "above the dome" (outside the Miniscus Layer, in what would be called "air") was and was not different from the water in liquid and frozen form.

The powerful effects of light and its absence affected all it touched. The Miniscus Layer, where the water fractals in vapor form touch the surface tension "Dome" of the liquid and solid water fractals is a symphony of movement. There, trillions times trillions times trillions of whirling molecular Vienna waltzes may each be as visible to God as the wheeling of solar systems throughout the universe.

There is beauty in the transformation into the solid state. Who has not marvelled at the irregular regularity of a snowflake? Who hasn't admired the fractal patterns of frost racing across glass? Those same patterns, and more, exist within ice, in a world so beautiful we cannot imagine it. Pain is there, too. According to Dante, ice is what God chose to lock souls in place in the lowest levels of the Inferno. "Like straws in glass.", they are trapped in an endless agony of frostbite.

There is magic in the Miniscus. The surface of a placid pond has a miniscus layer upon which water bugs can dance. As soon as someone throws a rock into the pond, each tiny droplet that arcs through the air instantaneously forms its own miniscus that keeps it together until the micro-second that it drops back beneath the greater miniscus of the pond that spawned it. Instantaneously, it loses its own identity with what seems an eager joy to again be part of the larger body. Oh, that we could join ourselves to God with as little concern for our individual selves.

Important: In water, the difference between form and substance is, for the first time, made clear. The incredibly complicated interplay between the three forms (solid, liquid, vapor) in one substance (water) remind us of something to be revealed later.

Water is more complicated than light, but less basic. Its form is often caused by light, but its substance is separate from it.

Then God said, "Let the water under the sky be gathered into a single place, so that the dry land may appear." And so it happened: the water under the sky was gathered into its basin, and the dry land appeared. God called dry land 'earth'. The basin of the water, He called "the sea". And, God saw that it was good."

The absence of light was dark. The absence of water was no water. With water and land, He made something more complicated, an opposite that was not a negation. He made land, which would appear to be the opposite of water, and placed the two appropriately. The contrasting, binary-like pair of the first programming session, Light and Dark, were joined by the more complicated opposites of Water and Earth.

On this day, the various fractals (and/or, their subprogrammers) were formed that would make minerals. Many of these fractals would be formed in veins and layers interleaved and interwoven throughout other layers and veins of mineral fractals. The complicated surface tension part of the Water Program kept the water from filling more of the pores of earth than necessary for future types of programs to keep from becoming mush.

What's meant by the single basin? All the connecting oceans, tributaries, and lakes are in a single basin. They are joined with groundwater by capillary tendrils.. Thinking about the giant miniscus layer that surrounds the top and bottom of all the contiguous water in the world takes a huge amount of thought. Beginning to imagine it helps us to obtain a dim glimmer of how intelligent God is, because He can visualize it perfectly in every detail.

God knew that He would be forming a creature with Free Will. So, He programmed the Earth Minerals carefully. He formed them into structures whose age and origin could not be determined by the coming Free Will Creature.

The Free Will Creature had to be free to choose whether or not the Earth was very old and the result of accidental causes. The Free Will Creature could also look at Creation, and choose to believe that the Bible's description of its origination was right. They would find patterns within the mineral fractals.

He may have used this Programming Session to arrange many of the layers of fossils. Free Will Creatures would be able to root around in them and freely choose to theorize from their findings how old they thought the world was. Truly, God has a sense of humor.

It may have been at this time that squads of angels programmed the continents and their shapes. "Make them move a little." were probable instructions. "Make them look as if a long time ago, they may have fit together. Let each generation of the Free Will Creatures to come be free to believe the Earth is as old as they want it to be." The brilliance of the stage setting lets us call ourselves "intellectual" for coming up with our own Theories About The Stage (science) and lets us give into the temptation of thinking that we're a lot smarter than we are.

This was the first time He considered His day's work and said He thought it was good. If He wasn't that pleased with the monumental tasks He'd already completed, can you imagine how little He is impressed with what we do on an ordinary day?

Then God said, "Let the earth bring forth vegetation: every kind of seed-bearing plant and every kind of fruit tree on earth that bears fruit with its seed in it." And so it was: the earth brought forth vegetation; every kind of seed bearing plant and every kind of fruit tree on earth that bears fruit with its seed in it. God saw how good it was. Evening came, and morning followed—the third day.

He programmed forms that could absorb energy, grow and reproduce their programming with what Iron-Age farmers called "seeds". We can more clearly understand their origin and purpose if we call them Replicating Multi-Dimensional Fractal Programs. God programmed light, water, and mineral fractals to support the first Replicating M-D Fractal Programs. They were designed to absorb fractal matter and movement and utilize the energy gained to aid in the development and propagation of their own unique fractal patterns.

Unmentioned in The Programming Archive are the tiny replicating fractals, viruses and other little life forms. They may have been programmed first, and used to quickly build more complicated plants. Or, the more complicated plants may have come first, and the small forms were taken from them, as Eve was taken from Adam.

Seeds are incredibly compact, portable programs that reproduce the fractal formulas that form them. Plant geneticists spend their careers working with miniscule parts of what God did on the third day.

Then God said: "Let there be lights in the dome of the sky, to separate day from night. Let them mark the times that are fixed, the days and the years, and serve as luminaries in the dome of the sky, to shed light upon the earth."

The dome of the sky is an atmospheric miniscus layer, beyond the denser air that gravity keeps in a thin shell around the Earth. After God programmed light, He programmed sub-programmers to program structures that would continuously emit and reflect light fractals. It was not enough to make light, He seems to have made what moderns might call giant light-generating/emitting diodes, and scattered them through the Void.

Again, this prefigures the coming of the Free Will Creature. If beings were to have Free Will, the light fractals would have to appear to emit from a source whose origin could not be quickly found by the limited intellectual abilities of the coming Free Will Creature. Even something that appeared to be as big and complicated as stars and planets had to be made so that their existence could be blamed on "accident".

This passage tells us there are two types of time. The Fixed Times are made of the days and years. These fixed times are divided into hours, minutes, and seconds. The Free Will Creatures could also compile them into decades, centuries, and millennia. Toward one end of the Fixed Time spectrum, time is fixed by the movements of the giant light-generating/emitting diodes. Towards the other end of that spectrum, time is fixed by the vibrations of cesium atoms.

The other kind of time, Unfixed Time, is a Time God uses. For Him, it's whatever time He wants. The sanest among us may hope that Unfixed Time may mean that a century in Purgatory may only take a few moments rather than a few millennia.

Souls living in Purgatory may be aware of time. "Only a little time left!", they may cry in relief. Souls in the Inferno or in Heaven may not be aware of time, although the souls in Hell before Christ descended to free them may have been, and probably were, comforted by the knowledge that He was on His way.

WHAT TIME IS IT?

The Sub-Programmer responsible for light did the job as directed. But, it went to his head, and he opened his own programming operation after convincing himself that his programming was just as good as anybody else's.

And so it happened: God made the two great lights, the greater light to govern the day, and the lesser one to govern the night: and He made the stars. God set them in the dome of the sky, to shed light upon the earth, to govern the day and the night, and to separate the light from the darkness. God saw how good it was. Evening came and morning followed—the fourth day.

At this point, God organized the light-bearers and makers to do more than just make light. He made them to move the light-emitting diodes and reflectors in stately fashion through the void, to provide rhythms for those programmed to need them, we who'd be looking up from below for guidance, and to automatically separate light from dark. Rhythms were also needed for the plant programs He'd spread all over the earth the Programming Session before last.   More than anyone, He knew they needed periods of alternating dark and light to grow.

He was preparing for the future programming of the Free Will Creatures who would need knowledge of the subtleties of time. His preparation for the man-form who was to come prefigured the prophets, who, in man-form, would also predict the God who was to follow.

He programmed structures that would program and emit light fractals as far away as the Free Will Creature could see. "The Free-Will Creatures must never be able to see an end to Creation, in either time or space." were likely instructions to the programmers and their subs. Otherwise, we wouldn't have the mental challenge of dealing with the God Who Is Infinite. If an end to Creation ever appeared, the chronic complainers among the Free Will Creatures could whine about "the pain of being created by a second-class programmer", and "the indignity of being forced to believe in a God Who is not infinite."

It is not an article of faith, but a supposition to be considered, that Creation may go on, both in galaxy-sized creations and in quark-sized creations, as far as Man can see just as soon as Man is able to see that far. It is a testimony to God's vastly superior intelligence that none of His creations contradict the Words He gave the first Free Will Creatures.

We can believe we live in a People-Centered Universe. A Current Technology Translation lets all ages see that a People-Centered Universe is possible. Believers believe that God made the universe for us. The Other Side wants us to believe that we are incidental occurrences in a Giant Accident.

This leads to what may be a Law Of Creation: God hates excessive inventory.

The Doctrine that God created a creation that adds on to itself as the vision of man is expanded by his microscopes and telescopes would indicate that God wants all ages to have an equal chance to find Him and be saved, but He provides this opportunity with a thrifty, Scotsman-like, minimum investment on His part.

He may not choose to waste valuable programming that isn't needed, if only to teach us the importance of thrift. It is plausible that He only has things created as necessary. When the first electron microscope was turned on, He'd had quarks already programmed to appear. When the Mount Palomar observatory went into operation, light from the Crab Nebulae arrived.

The idea that **God hates excessive inventory** leads to a big problem: How do we fit the seeming fact that we can see stars millions of light years away into a Creation Timetable only a few thousand years old?

One solution: Assume that God made the stars and the beams of light that radiate toward us from them at the same time. He may have set it up so that the rays would arrive at our retinas when they're supposed to.

In other words, Star X, one million light years away, was made simultaneously with a beam of light 999,995 light years long that appears to come from it.

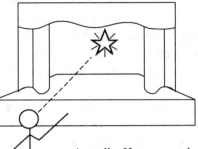

Actually, He may not have made Star X at all. He only has to make the beam of light for the star to appear to exist. He didn't have to make the beam any longer than He'd planned for the world to last. If we could get far enough beyond our current viewing position, could we see how long the beam is? Could we find out when the light would run out? Could we calculate The End? The Wise Men were able to calculate when the Old Testament would end. And, where.

Another way to look at it:

Sideways drawing of shaft of light, alternately appearing on and off.

Those who understand that it's possible that **God hates excessive inventory** are on the verge of this breakthrough: the beam only has to be there when people are looking at it. The lights may have been shut off in the daytime, before satellite observation and other advances forced the lights to be left burning.

Each beam may only be a few thousand light years long, and blinking off when no one's looking at it.

Right behind every shaft of starlight may not be a star, but the impending gloom of impending doom.

This notion that God hates excessive inventory leads to a modern version of the age old question, "If a tree falls in the forest and there's no one there to hear it, is there a noise?" Today's version: "If a tree falls in the forest and there's no one there, is there a tree? Is there a forest?"

Does the man who runs the movie projector show it to an empty house?

Then God said, "Let the water teem with living creatures. Let birds fly beneath the dome of the sky." And so it happened. God created the great sea monsters and all kinds of swimming creatures with which the water teems, and every kind of winged birds. God saw how good it was, and God blessed them, saying, "Be fertile, multiply, and fill the water of the seas; and let the birds multiply on the earth. Evening came, and morning followed—the fifth day.

Animals are Mobile Replicating Fractal Programs. They're more complicated than the portable multi-dimensional replicating programs (seeds) made earlier in the week. Each type of Replicating Fractal absorbs fractals produced by more primitive programs. The fox that eats the squirrel is more complex than the squirrel program that it eats. The squirrel has more lines of programming than the walnut program that it ingests which absorbs energy from the light, water, and mineral fractals allotted to its section of the Life Spectrum.

Iron-Agers divided Replicating Fractals Programs into "plants" and "animals", and laboriously classified them into species. Each Species Program is designed to gain energy from different parts of the energy spectrum. Each source of energy has Replicating Fractal Programs designed to absorb energy from it. The more complicated the Mobile Replicating Fractal Program (animal) is, the more sources of energy it can absorb.

On the other hand, each Species Program may have had a source of energy custom-designed for it. (Picture an angelic sub-programmer saying: "Look at this cute chipmunk! I've put it together out of left-over rat and gopher programs. Come up with a place for it to live, you guys in Fields and Forests!")

Swamps in the sun-drenched sub-tropics may be designed for cypress trees. Or, cypress trees may have been designed for sunny sub-tropical swamps. It may or may not matter which. But, each different Species Program is designed to access Energy Absorption Positions that differ in very slight degree. Naturalists call these Energy Absorption Positions "habitats".

The birds on the bird feeder are usually different from the species of birds on the ground below it. Each bird is programmed to take advantage of a unique situation that exists on its programmed level of Fractal Access.

Some birds will fly half-way around the world to find Energy Absorption Positions that allow Fractal Access. Scientists call this "migration".

Bird programs are the very first Mobile Replicating Fractal Programs that produced creatures capable of maintaining body temperatures far different from their surroundings. That is one reason people like to watch them.

Bird-watchers don't really watch birds. They are actually enjoying the complicated analysis required to understand a few visible aspects of the incredibly complicated Mobile Replicating Fractal Programs.

Birdwatchers rarely realize they are studying extraordinarily complicated Programs designed to absorb various lower types of Replicating Fractals. Programming of improved or different Fractal Access may continually take place. If so, this is the process called "evolution" by those who support the Conventional Reality Funding Structure so beloved by the Other Side.

Then God said, "Let the earth bring forth all kinds of living creatures: cattle, creeping things, and wild animals of all kinds." And so it was. God made all kinds of wild animals, all kinds of cattle, and all kinds of creeping things of the earth. And God saw that it was good."

Mammals are Mobile Replicating Fractal Formulae of a more complex nature. Like bird programs, they can maintain constant temperatures, and can therefore replicate their programs in more places on the earth fractals.

As with all the programs, many mammal-fractal programs feed on less complicated replicating fractal programs. Example: Cats eat mice. Wolves eat deer. Other animal fractal programs absorb energy from plant fractals in such large quantities that they must be mentally well organized enough to chase away smaller plant-eating fractal programs. Example: Herds of bison force antelope to the fringes of lush grasslands.

Warning: There are dangers in making a Current Technology Translation of the Bible based on technological improvements. The evils of the French Revolution, whose echoes continue to shout down the goodness of the individual, came about because four "New" Ways of looking at the world came into being:

The first of these four "New" Ways was increased skill at mechanics. As clocks became more complicated, and were miniaturized into watches, people began to look at animals as complicated, clockwork creatures. God was seen as little more than a Master Mechanic who had put in motion worlds that ticked away, as seen through the new optics, like a very complicated clock.

The new Mechanical Skills changed the way men saw themselves. Now, they were makers of their own creation. In their swollen conceits, many of them thought all creation looked like a process they could duplicate, if only they knew a little more. That made pre-destination seem plausible.

Calvin found that pre-destination, the second "New" Way used for evil, was an easy sell to an age that loved wind-up figures and gizmos. The problem with pre-destination is that it is, on some level, true. If God is one, His knowing and His willing are one.

That is not important to us. Our employer may know that we are going to be laid off in six months, but we still have to keep doing our job, if only for the references.

These two "New" Ways prompted one of the perpetual reappearances of Bacchus. This time, he used Rousseau. Rousseau had no morals, and he did what those who love evil always do: He said that, in this

"New" Way, morals were wrong. Good was bad. Bad was good. He said that "good" was only to be found in a "state of nature" in which it was "natural" for people to do whatever they felt like doing. There was no judge but ourselves, and our desires were our rightful king.

When this was instituted into government, collapse followed. Then, the pendulum swung from Rousseau's moral disorder and death to the excessive order and more death imposed by Napoleon's military machine. Lots of people died while the pendulum was at both ends of its swing.

The fourth "New" Way was the near-absolute success that Louis XIV had found in controlling France at the head of a huge bureaucracy empalaced at Versailles. The centralization of power he had achieved was remarkable. When the power of the Monarchy became both easily visible and concentrated, the power was seen as easily transferable.

The four "New" tributaries met, and turned to a flood of blood. Suddenly, power went to people proud of having no morals. They achieved mass communication with the print media spawned by new mechanical skills. The philosophers behind the power-grabbers told everyone who would listen that the world was a mechanical place in which men were only cogs. Once people were seen as pre-destined pawns, they were treated as expendable. People whose highest ideal was imposing their wills upon others looked at the mechanisms of Versailles, and saw that absolute rule could be theirs just as much as some King's.

We must be careful that a Current Technology Translation does not lead us away from the teachings of The Church. The Bible and The Church are the two legs upon which Christ stands upon Earth. The fact that Current Technology Translations may help us learn that Things may be made of Multi-Dimensional Fractal Programs does not mean that God's Creatures are not to be respected.

Even if living things of flesh and blood are built of mammothly complicated sub-programs, they still are God's Creatures. Familiarity must not breed contempt.

We must obey God and love our neighbor as ourselves. Whether we see our neighbor as an actor strutting on a stage, as a clockwork creature, as a hairless ape, or as a complicated Replicating Fractal Program, our neighbor is made in the image of God.

Our neighbor is our neighbor is our neighbor.

Then God said, "Let us make man in our image, after our likeness. Let them have dominion over the fish of the sea, the birds of the air, and the cattle, and over all the wild animals and all the creatures that crawl on the ground."

God created man in his image: in the image of God He created him; He created them male and female.

Replicating fractals increased in program complexity from day to day. On the sixth day of fractal creation, He made Man, the most complex of the Mobile Replicating Fractals.

WOW! LET'S CALL THEM COWS!

Man does more than simply ingest the less complicated programs below him. Man can harness fractal programs like oxen to pull plows made of entirely different fractals from the mineral family which he first forged and shaped using heat from plant fractals. Man can also use the fractal production capabilities of less intelligent fractal programs, allowing them to survive and multiply while helping man at the same time. Example: Man can take honey from bees, milk from cattle, wool from sheep.

"In the image of God" indicates that Man appears to have free will and some programming abilities. He could make and use tools. He could not fractalize directly, but he could work with fractal patterns. He could decide to obey or make up his mind to disobey.

In this passage, cattle are mentioned for the second time. He spent a lot of time working on the various cattle programs. Cattle would later provide tallow, hides, glue from hooves, as well as meat, milk, and power.

God blessed them, saying: "Be fruitful and multiply; fill the earth and subdue it. Have dominion over the fish of the sea, the birds of the air, and all the living things that move on the earth." God then said: "See, I give you every seed-bearing plant all over the earth and every tree that has seed-bearing fruit on it to be your food; and to all the animals of the land, all the birds of the air, and all the living creatures that crawl on the ground, I give all the green plants for food." And so it happened. God looked at everything he had made, and he found it very good. Evening came, and morning followed—the sixth day.

Do not be selfish, but bio-fractalize. Combine your own unique program with another unique program to produce even more unique programs. Organize and utilize the programs of all lower replicating and non-replicating fractal programs for the benefit of you and the ones you cause to be born after you.

All of Creation is there for men to use. There is no mention of worshipping any part of the Created World.

He thoroughly edited each of the programs. They worked together perfectly. There was no need for re-programming.

2

Thus the heavens and earth and all their array were completed. Since it was on the seventh day that God was finished with the work He had been doing, he rested on the seventh day from all the work He had done in creation. God blessed the seventh day, and made it holy because that was the day He rested from the work He had done during creation.

The basic programs had all been written and downloaded. Lesson for all who labor (program): After successfully completing a programming operation, one should rest. Each six days, one should complete a meaningful cycle of fractal activity, whether programming oneself, or providing sub-programming for more complex programmers. Example: Employers should figure out what needs to be done. Employees should do it.

One conclusion: There are seven classes of matter and movement.

The Second Story of Creation.

At the time when the LORD God made the earth and the heavens—-while as yet there was no field shrub on earth and no plants of the fields had sprouted, for the LORD God had not sent any rain upon the earth and there was no man to till the soil. But, a stream was welling up out of the earth and was watering all the surface of the ground—the LORD God formed man out of the clay of the ground, and blew into his nostrils the breath of life, and so man became a living being.

This fits in pretty well with the first story of Genesis. The plant fractals made on the third day were made in the form of seeds, and hadn't grown yet. The fact that they could they not have grown in only three days is a clue to the fact that the Earth was made in a short time, less than a week. Water hadn't had time to evaporate and form clouds to water the plant fractals long enough for them to grow.

The LORD God made hardware from silicon and other minerals. He programmed it with the most sophisticated software, a program that gave man the ability to utilize all the other fractal programs that had been created and gave man free will. In Man, hardware is different from software. In God, software is hardware.

Then, the LORD God planted a garden in Eden, in the east. There, He put the man whom He had formed. Out of the ground the LORD God made many species of trees to grow. They were beautiful to look at and good for food. The tree of life and the tree of the knowledge of good and evil were in the middle of the Garden.

The propensity that people have for private zoos and gardens reflects the similarity between God and we Free Will Creatures.

God made various refinements in plant fractalization, and put plants in the garden that were both beautiful and useful. He put the new Man in the biosphere where landscaping took place. Complicated fractals were developed that contained edible cellulose.

In the middle of the garden was the mathematical formula for life-fractals. Also in the middle was a formula that computed the consequences of disobeying The Instructions, but attempting to use it would automatically overload the man's circuitry and cause unavoidable errors.

With us, it is impossible that two things can occupy the same space. Yet, Scripture tells us that two trees are in the middle of the Garden. There can only be one middle, so both trees must be in the same space. The seeming impossibility that two trees were both in the middle of the garden could be explained through interwoven, shimmering fractals, vibrating much as do atoms above absolute zero, allowing lots of different things to be in the same exact Garden-Midpoint from microsecond to microsecond.

The mystery of two things in one place can also be solved by realizing that it is a clue to that fact that the formulae which make shapes take up neither space nor time. It also shows that the center of man's being is temptation.

A river is in Eden to water the garden. Beyond Eden, it divides into four branches. The first is Pishon; it is the one that winds through the whole land of Havilah, where there is gold. The gold of that land is excellent; bdellium and lapis lazuli are also there. The name of the second river is the Gihon; it is the one that winds all through the land of Cush. The name of the third river is the Tigris; it is the one that flows east of Asshur. The fourth river is the Euphrates.

There is, for the first time, a mention of things that have value in the human economy beyond food. The land in Havilah may have been as economically valuable as the gold, bdellium, and lapis lazuli that are mentioned. Land, gold, perfume, and jewelry are still rewards for successful programmers.

The main river may symbolize the Fractal Formulae for the fountain of life. It divides into four, one of which winds through a place where there are fractals of great value. Those fractals energize the other three, which may symbolize the three families of man that would survive the Flood.

The LORD God then took the man and settled him in the garden of Eden, to cultivate and care for it. The LORD God gave man this order: "You are free to eat from any of the trees of the garden except the tree of knowledge of good and evil. From that tree you shall not eat; the moment you eat from it you are surely doomed to die."

God took his most complicated program out of the laboratory and put it into Eden, a biosphere, a microcosm of earth, a private zoo. The man could not fractalize directly, but could deal with what had been pre-fractalized. He crudely manipulated that to get some of what he wanted. He was free to eat of the edible tree output. He had lots of excess processing capacity, but would overload and crash if he tried to download the huge Instruction Evaluation Program. Indeed, desiring to download a bigger program than he was capable of handling was an indication that willful corruption could take place if the man wanted it to.

Since the forbidden tree was in the middle of the Garden, Man may be being told not to go to the middle ground of any position. "The lukewarm water, I spit out of my mouth."

The LORD God said: "It is not good for the man to be alone. I will make him a helpmate." So the LORD God formed out of the ground different wild animals and various birds of the air. He brought them to the man to see what the man would call them. Whatever the man called each of them would be its name. The man gave names to all the cattle, all the birds of the air, and all the wild animals; but none proved to be the suitable partner for the man.

God made more complicated animals, to see how their RAM and ROM compared to the man's.

The man estimated the appearance, use, and capability of each, and labeled it accordingly. None even came close to the man's capacity. God spent a lot of time on cattle to provide maximum employment opportunities for future generations of man after the Biosphere phase.

God made different animals for the man, making up new formulae for replicating fractals that would be able to help the man. None of them were useful enough to be considered partners.

Most important lesson: Men should not try to use animals as partners. It's nice to have a dog or cat, but don't take it too seriously.

So the LORD God put a deep sleep on the man. While he was asleep, he took out one of his ribs and closed up its place with flesh. The LORD God then built up the rib that He had taken from the man into a woman. He brought her to the man, and the man said: "This, at last, is bone of my bones and flesh of my flesh. This one shall be called 'woman', for out of 'her man' this one has been taken."

That is why a man leaves his father and mother and joins himself to his wife, and the two of them become one flesh.

It was easy for God to modify the man's fractals by duplicating a disk copy, downloaded from a rib, the only bone in the man that would grow back, after being properly removed. After taking the fractals from the man's DNA program, they could be purified and refined.

By giving the Free Will Creature new animals to name, God had seen how the Free Will Creature responded to refined subtleties. He seemed to want a partner that the man would think he was free to choose.

The man realized that a comparable RAM/ROM being had been made with compatible chips and operating systems. Together, they could bio-fractalize life that would download parts of their individual programming. Neither of the programmed beings questioned their Programmer.

3

THE FALL OF MAN. Now the serpent was the most cunning of all the animals that the LORD God had made. It asked the woman, "Did God really tell you not to eat from any of the trees in the garden?" The woman replied to the serpent: "We may eat the fruit of the trees in the garden; it is only about the fruit of the tree in the middle of the garden that God said, 'You shall not eat it or even touch it, lest you die.' "But the serpent said to the woman: "You certainly will not die! No, God knows well that the moment you eat of it you will be like gods who know what is good and what is bad." The woman saw that the tree was good for food, pleasing to the eyes, and desirable for gaining wisdom. So she took some of its fruit and ate it; and she also gave some to her husband, who was with her, and he ate it. Then the eyes of both of them were opened, and they realized that they were naked; so they sewed fig leaves together and made loincloths for themselves.

God had programmed Things Unseen that usually operated in a more ethereal sphere. Some of them had the capability of doing very complicated programming, and one of them may have programmed the original Light Fractals. He may have been so pleased with himself that he thought that his programming ability was as good as The Programmer's. The computer virus did not try to corrupt the man's RAM. He knew that the man was too obedient.

He could tell that the woman was not as inclined to obedience. He crawled into the woman's mind by pretending to be her friend, got past the passwords, and began to get her to corrupt her program.

He did so by saying something he knew that the woman knew was wrong. "Did God say you shouldn't eat any fruit from any trees?" Women, who still love to correct mistakes, said "No, He never said that. What He said was that we shouldn't eat of the fruit from the tree in the middle of the garden." This was the opening the serpent needed.

"What? He thinks you aren't smart enough to download

the Big Program?" asked the virus. "No, we will crash." answered the woman. "No you won't. You're too smart for that. You'll just become more like The Programmer, and you'll be able to fractalize directly. You'll be just like us upper level Programmers.", he said. "I'd like that!", thought the woman. "I deserve it." She downloaded some of the program. She gave some to scan to her husband, who downloaded it, too.

This process of taking in an improperly accessed program and being corrupted by it may Prefigure by Opposition the transubstantiation of the Holy Eucharist.

Then, their eyes were opened, and they realized that they were no better than they were made. When they downloaded, they realized that The Programmer had not given them complete power to fractalize, but only to use materials that had been fractalized for them.

The portion of the program they downloaded allowed them to use crude tools to put things together. So, they attached fig leaves to each other and made crude clothes for themselves to cover the bio-fractalization ports that they thought were so much cruder than direct-fractalization methods used by the more ethereal life-fractals. They were ashamed of the very programming that had made them.

They heard the sound of the LORD God moving about in the garden at the breezy time of the day. The man and his wife hid themselves from the LORD God among the trees of the garden. The LORD God then called to the man and asked him, "Where are you?" He answered, "I heard you in the garden; but I was afraid, because I was naked, so I hid myself." God asked, "Who told you that you were naked? You have eaten, then, from the tree of which I had forbidden you to eat!" The man replied, "The woman whom you put here with me—she gave me fruit from the tree, and so I ate it."

The LORD God then asked the woman, "Why did you do such a thing?" The woman answered, "The serpent tempted me, so I ate it."

When they heard the sound of He Who Programmed All, they knew they'd done wrong. Parts of their programming worked well enough to let them know that they'd corrupted parts of their program. They tried to hide from The Programmer by blending in with the most complicated plant fractals. That showed their programs had been damaged badly enough that they no longer knew that nothing in Creation could hide from The Programmer. It proved they had free will.

The Programmer tested the complexity of His program by asking one question, and getting the answer to the question He really wanted. Since the Programming Journal mentions later that "all things work together for good", we can assume He was pleased that His most complicated program of the Free Will Creature worked. Despite owing everything to The Programmer, the man showed that he and the missus did have Free Will.

When the Free Will Creature said "I hid myself.", he was saying that there were at least two components of his being, one that could decide to hide and one that was hidden. The soul dragged the mind and body into the bushes?

The Programmer demanded to know where the virus had come from. The male sub-program could only let himself see immediate and external causes, and blamed his wife. She also only blamed immediate and external causes, alleging the fact that a very convincing virus caused the corruption.

Being tricked was not enough of an excuse. That meant that The Programmer had given them the power to have chosen not to let themselves be tricked. Neither the man nor the woman was much longer aware that they had permanently damaged their programs with the Original Glitch.

They did not realize that their programs had suffered an additional loss: they could no longer see clearly when something was their fault. Confession helps us restore our original programming.

Then the LORD God said to the serpent: "Because you have done this, you shall be banned from all the animals and from all the wild creatures; On your belly shall you crawl, and you shall eat dirt all the days of your life. I will put enmity between you and the woman, and between your offspring and hers; He will strike at your head, while you strike at his heel."

The Programmer changed the program of the Head Virus so that it could not have easy access to the way it moved around. "Your mobility and access to the Free Will Creatures shall be impeded. Your Operating Systems, and those whom you fractalize in your sub-programs, will be incompatible with the Operating Systems of the Free Will Creatures. They will destroy your RAM, ROM, and hardware while you can only attack them where they touch fractals of earth."

The Programmer is giving Future Free Will Creatures a message: "The only access that The Virus has is at your heel. This is symbolic: You can only become corrupted when you choose to come in contact with the lesser fractals. When you go beyond your program, you get into trouble. It is automatic. When you choose to sin, you begin the process of crashing, which starts with a small thing and quickly cascades into the Torrent of Pain."

To the woman, He said: "I will increase the pangs of your childbearing; in pain shall you bring forth children. Yet your urge shall be for your husband, and he shall be your master."

To the man He said; "Because you listened to your wife and ate from the tree of which I had forbidden you to eat, Cursed be the ground because of you! In toil shall you eat its yield all the days of your life. Thorns and thistles shall it bring forth to you, as you eat of the plants of the field. By the sweat of your brow shall you get bread to eat, Until you return to the ground from which you were taken; For you are dirt, and to dirt you shall return.

The man called his wife Eve, because she became the mother of all the living.

He gave a lesser punishment to the Women than to the The Virus. He told her: "You will have a harder time bio-fractalizing. Yet, your programming is being altered so that you will not deny your husband's desire to bio-fractal-ize."

The lesson is obvious: Willfully disobeying a superior programmer causes demotion.

The last to be punished was the man. He told the man, "Because you listened to a Sub-Programmer instead of to The Programmer, and downloaded a program I had restricted, you no longer have the power to access my pro-gram directly and just ask me to program what you want. You may now only exist by exerting physical force on less complicated fractals.

"You will not even be able to keep undesirable plant fractals from growing among the desirable plant fractals without physical effort. The difference between an edible plant and a weed is only a few molecules, but you will not even be able to rearrange them.

"You will work so hard that your evaporative cooling system will be engaged in order to maintain your crude fractal manipulation activities. You will spend your whole operating time working until you are defractalized into components."

The man called the other Free Will Replicating Fractal Eve, because all such others were made through her. When we ask why the first syllable of "evening" becomes the beginning of life, it can be depressing.

For the man and his wife, the LORD God made leather garments, with which He clothed them. Then the LORD God said: "See! The man has become like one of us, knowing what is good and what is bad! Therefore, he must not be allowed to put out his hand to pick fruit from the tree of life also, and thus eat of it and live forever." The LORD God therefore banished him from the garden of Eden, to till the ground from which he had been taken. When he expelled the man, he settled him east of the garden of Eden; and he stationed the cherubim and the fiery revolving sword, to guard the way to the tree of life."

The Programmer took coverings from the cattle programs in which He'd invested so much programming time, and made them long-lasting and flexible. He dressed the free-will fractals in them. He said, "See, you know what programs work and which don't. You must not be allowed to download a program that would allow you to run forever." This implies that there is a Master Program, and that people can mess it up. The free-will Creatures could not live forever, they had to go to judgment. Powerful spirit-fractals, armed with a de-fractalizer, were stationed to protect the Main Programs from unauthorized downloading.

Another Current Technology Translation: A little boy and his friend have taken the father's car for a joy ride. His father finds them hiding in the garage. "So, you know how to start the car and steer it around. I'm taking away the credit card I'd let you use at the store. If I leave the credit card with you, you could drive around forever and get in all kinds of trouble. In fact, I'm not letting you anywhere near a source of credit. From now on, you can walk. If you want a bicycle, make one."

4

Cain and Abel. The man had relations with his wife Eve. She conceived and bore Cain, saying, "I have produced a man with the help of the LORD." Next she gave birth to his brother Abel. Abel became a keeper of flocks, and Cain a tiller of the soil. In time Cain brought an offering to the LORD from the fruit of the soil, while Abel, for his part, brought one of the best firstlings of his flock. The LORD looked with favor on Abel and his offering, but on Cain and his offering he did not. Cain greatly resented this and was crestfallen. So the LORD said to Cain: "Why are you so resentful and crestfallen? If you do well, you can hold up your head; but if not, sin is a demon lurking at the door: his urge is to destroy you, even so, you can be his master.

Adam and Eve bio-fractalized, and named their first Replicating Free-Will fractal formulation 'Cain'.

Everyone who reads this passage knows that it was not Adam, but Eve, who had the ego to immediately put herself on a near-par with The Programmer. Some think that The Programmer likes big egos. "I did it. God helped." The colossal ego of the First Woman was not diminished by the punishment described in a preceding chapter.

Soon, another Free Will Creature, Abel, was bio-fractalized. Abel could handle the more complicated animal fractals, particularly the cattle fractals on which The Programmer had lavished so much attention. Cain was a dirt farmer. He was able to stick seeds in the ground and pull weeds while he waited for the plants to produce food.

When they brought the results of their tiny programs to The Programmer, He was more impressed with Abel's than Cain's.

Cain thought his programs were just as good as Abel's. When he found they weren't, he lowered his head (programming unit).

The Programmer said: "Are you mad just because your brother can program better than you can? If you are happy with your programming ability, and are grateful for it, you can hold your programming unit high. But, if you can't be happy and grateful for your ability, one of The subViruses trying to get into your programming unit will do so. He's trying to get in and destroy you, but your programming is strong enough to keep him out if you choose to keep him out."

Cain may have symbolized everyone who would ever be envious.

Cain said to his brother Abel, "Let us go out into the field." When they were in the field, Cain attacked his brother Abel and killed him. Then the LORD asked Cain, "Where is your brother Abel?" He answered, "I don't know. Am I my brother's keeper?" The LORD then said: "What have you done! Listen: Your brother's blood cries out to me from the soil! Therefore you shall be banned from the soil that opened its mouth to receive your broth-er's blood from your hand."

The envious, less intelligent of the Free-Will Replicating Fractal patterns enticed his brother away from the others. Then, the envious programmer killed the smarter one. The Programmer asked the murderer where his brother was.

Cain, like his Father when caught in sin, tried to hide. He may have been smarter than Adam because he knew enough not to physically hide. He hid behind a lie, and said he didn't know. Then, he cleverly tried to distract The Programmer with a philosophical question. (He might have heard the smarter mini-programmers talking with The Programmer in such a fashion. He didn't understand it, but could make the same sounds.) The Programmer already knew what had happened. The process of de-frac-talization was audible to Him. When He heard the compli-cated blood fractals breaking apart, He was angry.

"I can still hear the blood de-fractalizing in the dirt! Therefore, you shall be banned from the soil that absorbed the components of those fractals you put there when you began the defractalization process. Because you spoiled both the Abel Program and the soil program, you can no longer even be a dirt farmer. You'll just have to wander around trying to find a terminal." And, Cain had tried to fool God, to get Him off the track with a silly question. God didn't like that. When He asked "What have you done?", He was asking, "Haven't you killed your brother and lied to me? Tried to fool me? You have chosen to be really stupid."

Cain said to the LORD: "My punishment is too great to bear. Since you have now banished me from the soil, and I must avoid your presence and become a restless wanderer on the earth, anyone may kill me at sight." "Not so!" the LORD said to him. "If anyone kills Cain, Cain shall be avenged sevenfold." So the LORD put a mark on Cain, lest anyone should kill him at sight. Cain then left the LORD'S presence and settled in the land of Nod, east of Eden.

Cain said to The Programmer: "I can't stand that much de-programming. Please don't treat me as if I'm as stupid as I was. Since you have taken me from my simple plant fractals, and I have to stay away from you so that I can't even be de-bugged, and wander from terminal to terminal, anyone may de-program me to the point of de-fractalization when they see me." "No, they can't.", The Programmer told him. If anyone deprograms or defractalizes you, they'll be punished with seven times as much."

This must mean that there are fates worse than death. In this case, seven times worse than death. This is the first mention of punishment beyond the field of Directly Known Programming. Until now, the worst punishment Cain could think of was having death visited upon him.

The Programmer assured him, and us, that there were things a lot worse than death, or, being de-programmed. The Programmer put a lockout on Cain's CPU to protect him. Cain then left The Programmer, and went to a state of partial shutdown away from the Main Programs.

Fittingly, in the land of Nod.

So?

Translating God's Word in terms of Current Technology, even to ourselves, helps us see how real the Bible is. Then, we can tell our friends and neighbors. Applying some of the thinking in this book will help us and others get closer to God.

Why is that so important? As people draw closer to God, they stop lying and believing in lies. All problems in families, communities and nations begin with lies. Solutions to problems can only be found when we love and seek truth.

At the end of our time on earth, each one of us will go to judgment. If, during our allotted time, we have led another person closer to God, we will have covered up a multitude of our own sins.

Horrible pain can be avoided.

Portersville, Pennsylvania. 1997

William E. Adams was born and raised in Illinois. Attended St. Bede, where he discovered Chesterton. Graduated from Ripon College, then Officer's Candidate School at Ft. Benning. Served in the United States and South Vietnam.

Received degree in Library Science, worked as a children's Librarian. That gave him an opportunity to learn the Fairy Tales as an adult. He started to believe them. He resigned his tenured position and started a business with a ten thousand dollar inheritance.

Today, Adams Mfg. is the largest producer of suction cups in the world. Bill has over fifty patents. His company manufactures household and consumer products, and provides hundreds of jobs in the United States.

Bill is a conservative, and has been re-elected to his School Board, which has the lowest taxes in his County.

"It's a lot harder to lower taxes than it is to invent and sell new products." Bill discovered.

"My Yoke is Easy . . ." is Bill's third book.

The only way that most of your family, friends, and neighbors will find out about *My Yoke is Easy, and My Burden is Light* will be if you give them a copy.

You'll be buying them presents, anyway. Get something good for them.

If a person reads *My Yoke is Easy . . .* and is moved even *slightly* closer to seeing how reasonable faith is, they get closer to God and you build up Heaven Credits. If you help.

Remember how much a few important books helped you? Seeing that Faith is reasonable is the very first step for many who haven't gotten as far as you.

"My Yoke is Easy" is a perfect gift for young people whom you love. How else will they ever see how reasonable our beliefs are, when everything we hold Holy is attacked every day of their lives?

Talk to others about "My Yoke is Easy . . ." Lend your copy or order another for a special friend or relative. One by one, two by two. That's how we change the world.

Books by Bill Adams
from Old Drum Publishing:

My Yoke is Easy, and My Burden is Light ...

112 pages. Illustrated. $6.95

Even people who've studied Scripture for years don't know what
"my burden is light" means. They won't know until you tell them.
This exciting theory of Bible Translation shows that Science is the
handmaiden of Faith. Puts beginners ahead of many " experts " when
it comes to bringing moderns closer to God. Revolutionary ideas
about the origin and structure of matter.

CRATS!

360 pages $6.95

A Pilgrim's Progress for our times. Modern pilgrimages through the
murderous lunacy of Government programs to the peaceful sanity of
the Church. Introduces the concept that our ancestors began in The
Twelve Tribes. Points out that Conventional Reality is just that.

Combining free will and fractals makes credible the idea that
Creation is only a few thousand years old. Fossils were made in place
to let people choose to believe in God or in accidents.

Guarantee: When you've finished, you'll be able to explain how
real, live camels can go through the eyes of needles. What many think
of as 'bizarre' parts of the Bible seem reasonable. "Prophetic."

All the World is a Stage.

135 pages. Illustrated $6.95

Simplifies the needless complexity of modern political/business/
scientific/social theory. The World is, or can be seen as, a Stage.

The only two things on The Stage are Props and Actors. Props may
be made out of 3-D Fractals that God or His angels programmed.
There are two kinds of Props.

Actors are creatures who appear to have Free Will. Actors only
have a couple of dozen kinds of jobs. Each Actor is in one of three
Guilds.

The notion of an Invisible Producer with Programming skills helps
make sense out of all that is thought to be known.

Telephone orders: Call, toll free, 1-800-OLD-DRUM. Please have Visa/MC ready.
Fax orders: (412) 368-3339 Other calls, 1(412) 368-3338.

Postal orders: **Old Drum Publishing**, Box 401, Portersville, Pa 16051-0401 USA

Name _____

Address _____

City _____ State _____ Zip _____

Phone_____

Please send the following books:
(I understand that I am able to return books for a refund, no questions asked)

    Title: _____ #of copies _____ @ $6.95 = _____

    Title: _____ #of copies _____ @ $6.95 = _____

    Title: _____ #of copies _____ @ $6.95 = _____

    Shipping $3.00 for the first book
    and $1.00 for each additional book.   Shipping: _____

PA residents please add 6% for books shipped to PA address.   Total _____

Method of payment: _____Check _____Visa _____Mastercard

Card Number: _____ Expiration Date: _____ / _____

Name on card: _____

Quantity discounts make these books great gifts. You'll be buying presents, anyway. Get something good for people you like. 12 books (mix or match) $5.00 per book. Add $6.00 for shipping.

Telephone orders: Call, toll free, 1-800-OLD-DRUM. Please have Visa/MC ready.
Fax orders: (412) 368-3339 Other calls, 1(412) 368-3338.

Postal orders: **Old Drum Publishing**, Box 401, Portersville, Pa 16051-0401 USA

Name _____

Address _____

City _____ State _____ Zip _____

Phone_____

Please send the following books:
(I understand that I am able to return books for a refund, no questions asked)

    Title: _____ #of copies _____ @ $6.95 = _____

    Title: _____ #of copies _____ @ $6.95 = _____

    Title: _____ #of copies _____ @ $6.95 = _____

    Shipping $3.00 for the first book
    and $1.00 for each additional book.   Shipping: _____

PA residents please add 6% for books shipped to PA address.   Total _____

Method of payment: _____Check _____Visa _____Mastercard

Card Number: _____ Expiration Date: _____ / _____

Name on card: _____

Quantity discounts make these books great gifts. You'll be buying presents, anyway. Get something good for people you like. 12 books (mix or match) $5.00 per book. Add $6.00 for shipping.

Reader Comments

"Three hundred years ago, Blaise Pascal invented Probability Theory and applied it to wagering. Then he applied it to choosing which way to wager the Big Bet, whether or not God is real. Pascal made it easier to bet smart."

"Today, Bill Adams has developed the concepts of Multi-Dimensional Fractals and Current Technology Translation. He uses both ideas to show that the Bible's account of Creation is reasonable. Adams makes it easier to find God."

Reader

L et us know what <u>you</u> think of *My Yoke is Easy . . .*

_____

_____

_____

_____

_____

_____

_____

_____

_____

_____

_____

All comments become the property of Old Drum Publishing